GW01191235

London Borough of Merton

M00876645

COMIC STRIP SCIENCE ADVENTURES

DIGGING FOR DINOSAURS

Paul Mason and Jess Bradley

I'm back – and I'm still the BIGGEST!

WAYLAND

First published in Great Britain in 2025
by Wayland

Copyright © Hodder and Stoughton, 2025

All rights reserved

Editor: Sarah Peutrill
Designer: Rocket Design (East Anglia) Ltd
Text consultant: Dr Dave Hone

HB ISBN: 978 1 5263 2721 5
PB ISBN: 978 1 5263 2723 9
Ebook ISBN: 978 1 5263 2722 2

Printed and bound in China

Wayland, an imprint of
Hachette Children's Group
Part of Hodder and Stoughton
Carmelite House
50 Victoria Embankment
London EC4Y 0DZ

An Hachette UK Company
www.hachette.co.uk
www.hachettechildrens.co.uk

The authorised representative in the EEA is Hachette
Ireland, 8 Castlecourt Centre, Castleknock Road,
Castleknock, Dublin 15, D15 YF6A, Ireland

MIX
Paper | Supporting
responsible forestry
FSC
FSC® C104740

CONTENTS

UNCOVERING DINOSAURS

Millions of years ago, dinosaurs ruled the Earth – but if they died out millions of years ago, how do we know that? It's because of their remains, called fossils.

WHAT WERE DINOSAURS?

Dinosaurs were reptiles – the group of animals that today contains crocodiles, snakes and lizards, for example. Among their most important features were:

• dinosaurs had legs that allowed them to stand upright.

• dinosaurs (like some other reptiles) had two holes behind their eye sockets. Muscles that passed through these holes gave them a stronger bite.

FINDING FOSSILS

Fossils are the bone-stone remains of dead dinosaurs*. Every year, new fossils are discovered that tell us more about what dinosaurs were like. For instance, dinosaurs used to be drawn with scaly, lizard-like skin. We now know, though, that some of them had feathers.

*Bone that turned to stone: find out how this happened on page 10.

FOSSIL-HUNTING ADVENTURES

Fossil hunting can be an adventurous (and dangerous) business. Fossil hunters have experienced extreme cold and heat, sandstorms, danger from bandits and explosions.

Today's fossil hunters are much better behaved, and it's been ages since any of them threw rocks at each other.

STORMY DISCOVERIES

Mary Anning was born in 1799 and, despite having hardly been to school, she became one of the world's first great fossil hunters.

Mary starts fossil hunting with her dad.

Is this a good one?

We'll clean it and see.

The best hunting is after winter storms, which uncover new fossils.

When Mary is 11, her father dies.

Richard Anning 1766–1810

Mary and her brother Joseph take over the fossil hunting.

Seen anything?

Not even ammonites!

NOW we've found something, Mary!

Not bad for a 12-year-old.

Mary finds and digs out the rest of the skeleton. It is 5 metres long!

Anyone got any fish? I'm starving.

Ichthyosaur

Mary's family sells the ichthyosaur for £23.

Thank you, sir.

It will look great in the collection.

Mary keeps looking for fossils.

Come on, boy.

BARK!

Her dog Tray comes too.

1823: Mary uncovers the first-ever plesiosaur skeleton.

No one has seen anything like it before.

At first not everyone agreed that the fossil was real ...

Impossible! It was found by a WOMAN!

It IS real!

... but in the end:

GEOLOGICAL SOCIETY

Yes, OK – it is real.

Mary's work is dangerous. In 1833, she's almost killed by a landslide.

RUMBLE!

CRASH!

Watch out!

Tray is not so lucky.

Tray! No!

He is crushed to death.

Mary becomes so well known that famous scientists ask her advice.

Let's talk fossils!

Err, OK.

Could these stones be ... dinosaur poo?

They could!

In fact, they are!

Scientists name the stony dino poo 'coprolite.'*

* Women weren't *really* allowed to name science things back then.

Mary becomes ill and dies in 1847. She is just 47 years old.

Mary Anning 1799–1847

Her friend Henry De la Beche creates a painting that imagines the world Mary had uncovered.

HOW FOSSILS FORM

We know about dinosaurs because of fossils — but what actually are fossils, and how do they form?

To understand, let's imagine an ordinary dinosaur such as a *Triceratops*. *Triceratops* is going about its everyday life ...

Suddenly, *Triceratops'* day goes badly wrong.

Soon, all that is left of *Triceratops* is bones.

Triceratops' bones are covered by a layer of mud then, over millions of years, more mud, sand and even volcanic ash. These eventually are squashed down and become hard rock.

As this was happening, water seeped into *Triceratops'* bones. Minerals from the water turned the bones to stone.

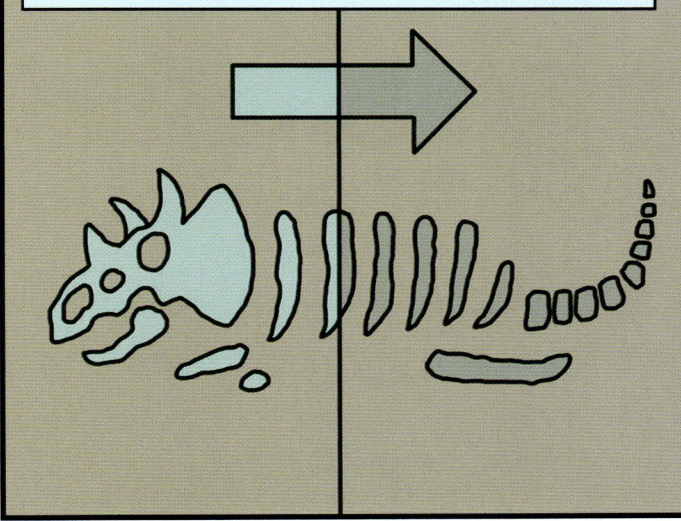

As Earth changed over time, the rocks where *Triceratops* was buried lifted up to the surface.

Woo hoo! A dinosaur!

Finally, millions of years after it had died, someone saw a bit of *Triceratops* sticking out of the ground – and dug out the rest.

THE BONE WARS

Today's fossil hunters are (mostly) well-behaved palaeontologists and their helpers. Not so long ago, though, fossil hunters behaved so badly that they caused the 'Bone Wars.'

Millions of years ago, North America:

There are dinosaurs everywhere — and some will become fossils.

1800s, USA: two palaeontologists lead the hunt for new dinosaurs ...

One was very wealthy: Marsh's millionaire uncle built him a museum.

It's just what I needed.

Othniel C Marsh

The other was quite wealthy: Cope inherited about £250,000.

It was a lot of money back then!

Edward Drinker Cope

At first they were friends and even went fossil hunting together ...

We've found loads of fossils here.

Thanks for showing me.

... but they were also rivals.

I'll pay you to send fossils to me, not him.

The two soon disagreed about how dinosaurs developed.

They changed really slowly!

No they didn't!

They disagreed about what prehistoric animals should be called.

I name this creature *Tinoceras!**

I name it *Loxolophodon!*

*It's actually called *Uintatherium* and had already been named by someone else.

And when Cope wrongly described a new fossil ...

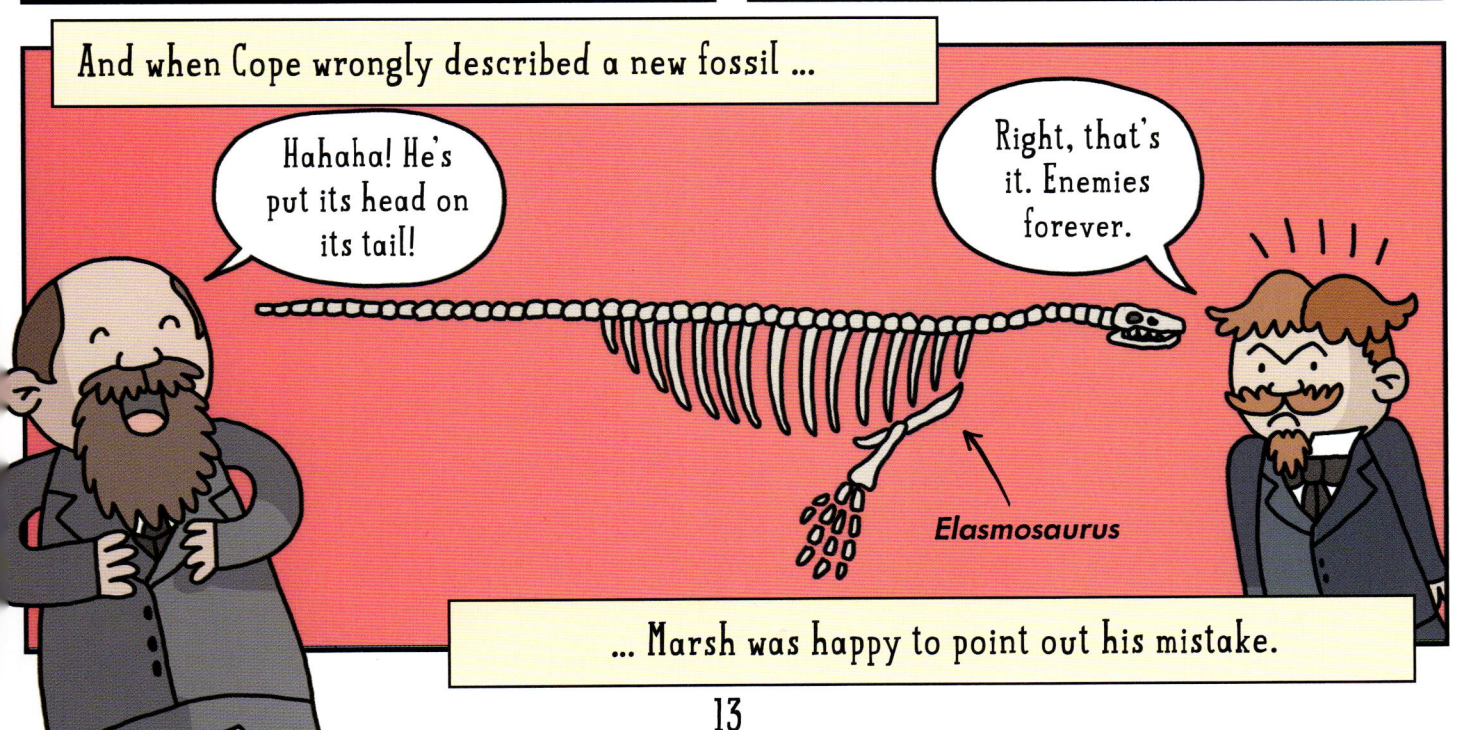

Hahaha! He's put its head on its tail!

Right, that's it. Enemies forever.

Elasmosaurus

... Marsh was happy to point out his mistake.

Meanwhile in Wyoming, in 1877:

These must be valuable.

Let's write to that rich professor.

William Reed

William Carlin

Marsh employs Reed and Carlin as fossil hunters.

WHOO-O-WOO!

Wagonloads of fossils are soon heading east.

By December, *Stegosaurus*, *Allosaurus* and *Apatosaurus* have all been unearthed.

Nice to meet you.

GRRRR!

Ignore her.

The *Laramie Daily Sentinel* publishes news of the digging.

Laramie Daily Sentinel

NEW DINOSAUR DISCOVERIES

Reed and Carlin Unearth Bones

Cope immediately sends 'dinosaur rustlers' to the area ... and persuades Carlin to work for him.

SNORE! SNORE!

This way.

I was persuaded by the money.

Carlin locks Reed out of the local train station.

COMO BLUFF TRAIN STATION

That'll fix him ...

Reed has to pack the bones on the train platform in the bitter cold.

Is that fossils clanking?

It's my teeth chattering.

*Possibly.

The two teams of fossil hunters even fight by throwing rocks at each other.*

OUR bones!

WHIZZ!

CRASH!

CLONK!

They're OURS!

Both sides are desperate to stop the others finding new fossils.

Just make sure Cope/Marsh* doesn't get them.

The fossil hunters smash up fossils ...

CRASH! CRUNCH!

*delete as needed.

... they fill quarries with rocks and earth ... and even blow them up using dynamite.

Haven't we only just dug this hole?

BOOM!

I prefer doing it this way.

Yes, much easier.

Conditions were tough for the fossil hunters.

Pass some water.

It's like an oven out here.

After almost dying in a freezing blizzard, one of Marsh's fossil hunters resigned ...

... and returned to his old job, teaching.

Honestly, this is safer.

The Bone Wars ended in the 1890s.

DINOSAUR EXPLORATION EXCAVATION

Closed for Business

Cope and Marsh had run out of money.

16

By the 1890s, both their reputations were trashed ...

Read all about it!

SCIENTISTS AT WAR

... and palaeontology was less respectable than it used to be.

And what do you want to be when you grow up?

A palaeontologist.

Mum faints →

By the time the Bone Wars were over, Marsh and Cope had described 136 American dinosaurs.*

Stegosaurus (Marsh)

Ornithomimus (Marsh)

Brontosaurus (Marsh)

Allosaurus (Marsh)

Camarasaurus (Cope)

Coelophysis (Cope)

*Although today only about 40 of Cope and Marsh's names are still used.

REVEALING FOSSILS

Fossils are bone that have turned to stone. They are surrounded by rock, so getting them out can be quite a challenge.

Some fossils are surrounded by much softer rock that is easily removed. For trickier fossils, there are two main ways of removing rock.

1. CHIPPING AND DRILLING

If a fossil is inside hard rock, the rock has to be carefully chipped and drilled away.

A hammer and chisel is used to remove larger pieces.

An air pen is used to remove smaller pieces.

For some fossils, a microscope and tiny drill then remove the remaining fragments ...

Ta-dah!

2. ACID BATHS

Soft rock such as limestone or chalk can be removed using an acid bath — plus a LOT of patience.

I'm not sure I want an acid bath.

First the rock is placed in weak acid for 1–3 days.

Actually that's not too bad.

Next the rock stands under running water for three times as long.

This is a very long shower.

Each time, only 1–3 mm of rock is removed.

Am I ever going to get out of here?

After months or years, the fossil is finally revealed.

Woo hoo! Free at last!

SAD STORY OF A *SPINOSAURUS*

Spinosaurus was a big – really big – fish-eating dinosaur from North Africa. The first *Spinosaurus* ever discovered was ... well, 'unlucky' probably doesn't cover it.

Egypt, 100 million years ago.

Feeling a bit peckish ...*

*Spinosaurus is nearly always peckish.

Argh! Urgh! Ow!

Num, num.

CHOMP! MUNCH!

Spinosaurus LOVES fish.

Not ONLY fish, though ...

SNIFF! SNIFF!

Spinosaurus sometimes steals other dinosaurs' dinner.

RAA-AAR!

AAAAGH!

In 1912, Spiny finally makes it back to the light.

What's this?

Fossils!

At last!

The fossil hunter in charge realises Spiny could be important ...

Hmm. This looks important.

... so he sends the fossils to his boss in Munich, Germany.

To: E STROMER, MÜNCHEN, GERMANY

CONTENTS: UNKNOWN DINOSAUR

Sender: R Markgraf, Egypt

Delivery for Herr Professor Stromer.

Oooh, exciting!

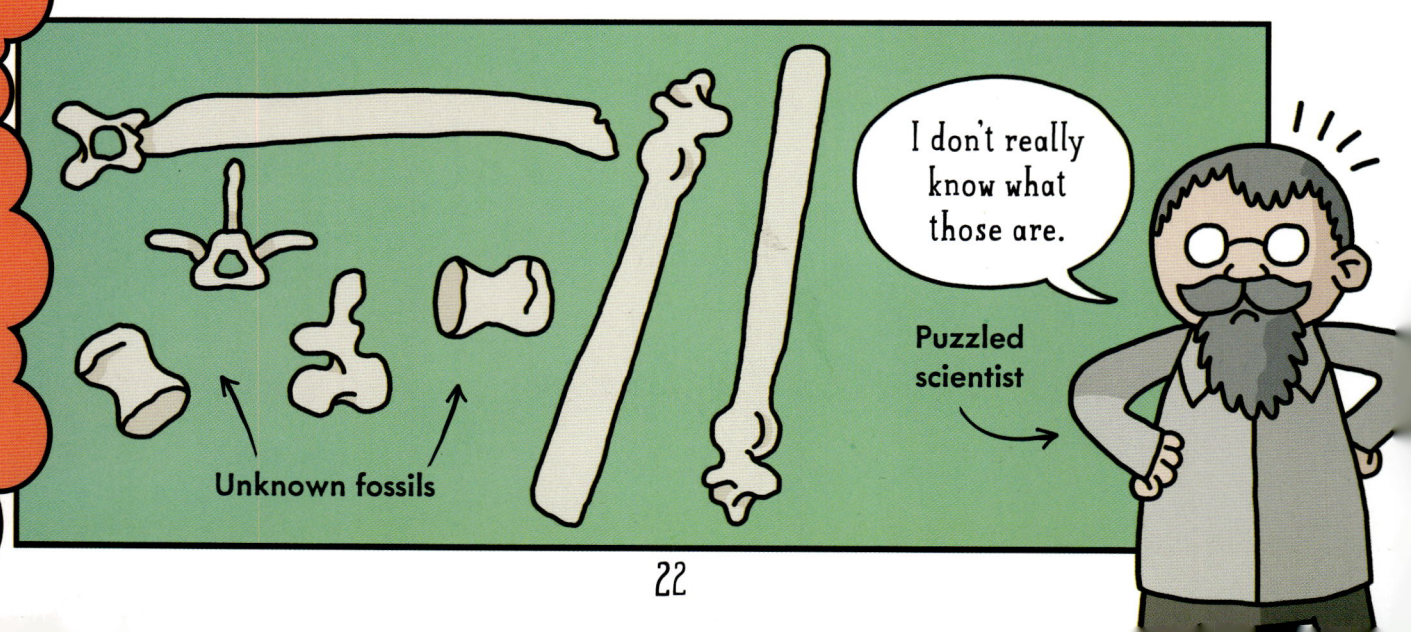

I don't really know what those are.

Unknown fossils

Puzzled scientist

Spiny ends up living in a museum in Munich, Germany.

I hear it's good.

All the way from Africa!

Terrifying, they say.

This is a long queue.

Shall we go to the park instead?

Stromer does the best he could to imagine what Spiny once looked like.

RAA-AAR!

He didn't do a brilliant job, to be honest.

As if THAT isn't bad enough, Spiny's troubles aren't over yet ...

In 1939, the Second World War begins, after Germany invades Poland.

Watch out!

Later, German cities are bombed.

Munich was one of the cities that is hit.

The museum where Spiny lived is almost destroyed.

Has anyone seen my dinosaur?

Spiny is never seen again.

SAD STORY OF A SPINOSAURUS

About 40 years later, one of Spiny's cousins are unearthed.

Hel-looo. I'm *Baryonyx*, from England.

Remind you of anyone?

Then, in Morocco, there is another important discovery:

What's this?

A *Spinosaurus*. of course.

So when we compared the two skulls ...

Baryonyx skull

Hey, Spiny!

Cousin Barry!

Spinosaurus skull

... we realised they must have been similar dinosaurs.

And you know what? We actually were.

So even though Spiny is long gone, his relatives are still with us.

CRACKING THE *OVIRAPTOR* CASE

New science is constantly changing our understanding of dinosaurs – as the case of *Oviraptor*, the 'egg thief', shows.

The desert is a tough place to explore. In the day it's boiling hot.

There's hardly any water.

At nighttime it's freezing.

Violent sandstorms appear with almost no warning.

During one expedition, the storms hardly stopped for six weeks.

The fossil hunters are looking for the remains of early humans ...

Found anything?

Not yet.

... but they find something else.

Hang on!

Yes – they found me!

Protoceratops (not an early human ...)

Despite the tough conditions, the fossil hunters also discover other dinosaurs.

Velociraptor

Nice to meet you.

They also find dinosaur eggs.

Proof, at last!*

* This was the first proof that dinosaurs laid eggs.

People everywhere are fascinated by the news.

Could dinosaur eggs hatch?

Meanwhile, back in the desert:

We're lost again, aren't we?

Possibly.

While Andrews asks for directions ...

We're looking for the army base.

... there's a discovery nearby. A LOT of fossils.

Andrews! Come and see.

Winter is coming, so the fossil hunters head home ...

... but they vow to come back next year.

Back home, an egg auction helps pay for the next expedition.

Shall we start the bidding?

Dinosaur egg

SOLD! for ... $5,000.

Surprised

BANG!

Pleased

When the fossil hunters return, they find more dinosaurs.

SCRAPE! SCRAPE!

One is a small dinosaur on top of some eggs.

People imagine it had been stealing *Protoceratops'* eggs ...

Oi! Bring that back.

... and it's named *Oviraptor*, or 'egg thief'.

In 1993, an investigation of eggs from the Gobi reveals a surprise.

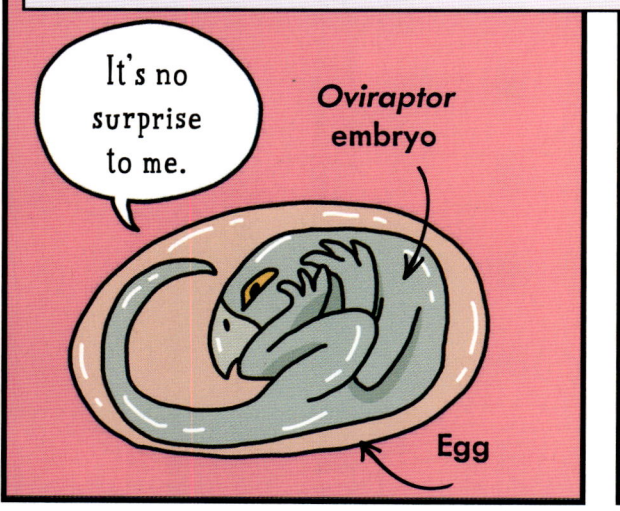

It's no surprise to me.

Oviraptor embryo

Egg

If those are *Oviraptor* eggs...

Oviraptor wasn't an egg thief at all!

Oviraptor had been guarding its own eggs, not stealing someone else's.

Then disaster struck ...

Oh no! A sandstorm.

... *Oviraptor* stayed with its eggs and was buried with them.

80 million years* later, the fossils were dug up and the 'egg thief' was unfairly named.

As if being buried alive wasn't bad enough.

*More or less.

Now we know the truth. *Oviraptor* actually tried to look after its eggs.

Stacey, come back!

Not likely.

The dinosaur was actually just being a good parent.

THE EIGHT-MILLION-DOLLAR DINOSAUR

About 67 million years ago in South Dakota, USA*, there lived a dinosaur that would one day be worth millions of dollars.

*Which wasn't called that back then.

1990: fossil hunters in South Dakota are heading home …

There's something wrong with the truck …

… but there's a delay.

Flat tyre

Time for one last look around.

I won't be long!

Sue Hendrickson, fossil hunter

Hmm – these look interesting.

Dinosaur backbones

The fossil hunters had found something big. Really big.

The fossil hunters had found a *T. rex*. They named it Sue.

Sue

Sue? SUE?

Sue

Seventeen days later:

Let's get Sue inside for a clean-up.

STOP calling me Sue!

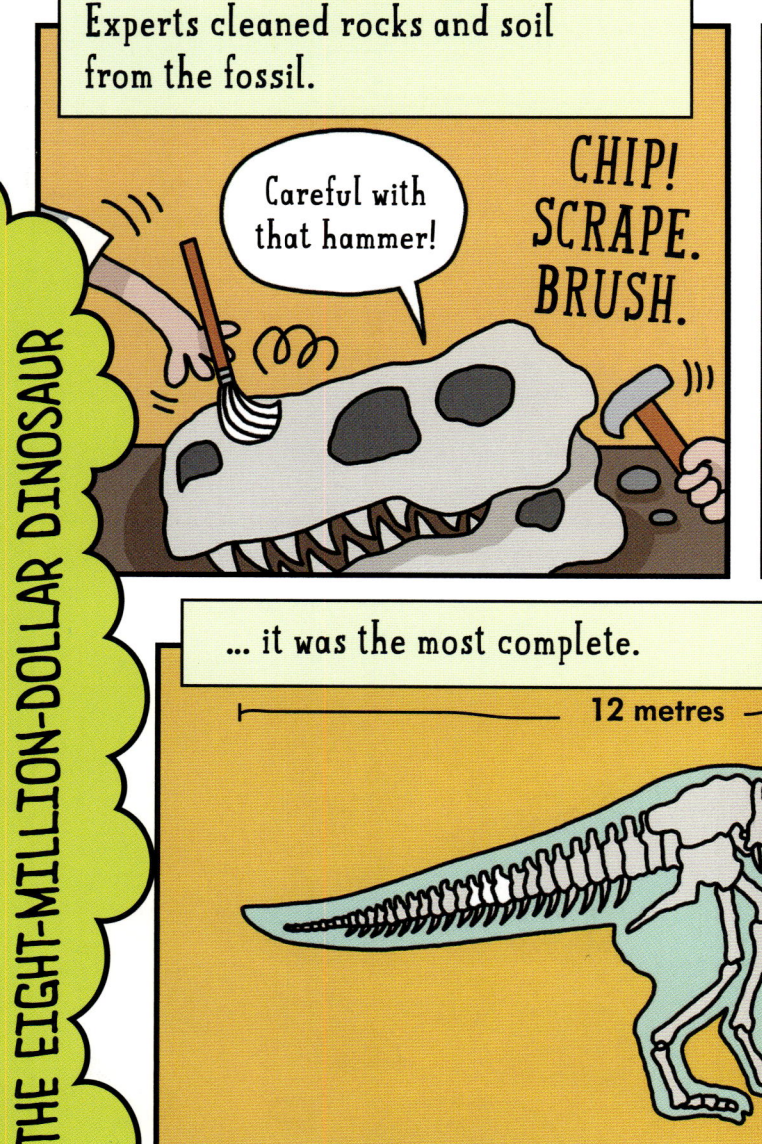

Experts cleaned rocks and soil from the fossil.

Careful with that hammer!

CHIP! SCRAPE. BRUSH.

Not only was Sue the biggest *T. rex* yet found ...

Look, my name's not Sue. It's ... actually, I can't remember.

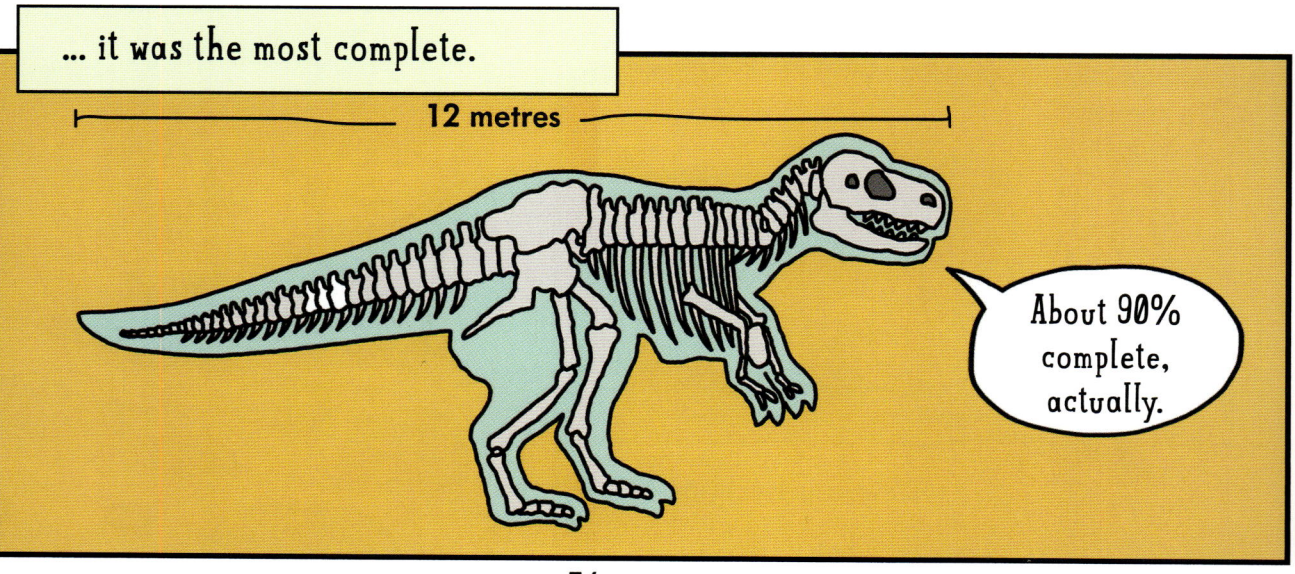

... it was the most complete.

12 metres

About 90% complete, actually.

Years later, Sue was put up for sale.

For Sale By **AUCTION**

4 October 1997 in NEW YORK CITY

The *TYRANNOSAURUS REX* known as **'Sue'**

Bring LOTS of money.

Bidding started at $500,000 ...

He better not call me Sue.

... and 10 minutes later:

Sold! For $7.6 million: Specimen FMNH PR 2081.

Actually, Sue's not a bad name.

BANG!

The winner was the Field Museum in Chicago.

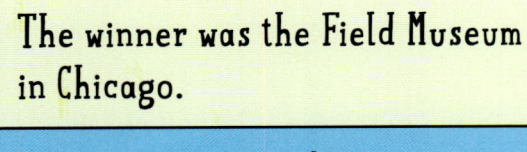

Chicago

You've bought a WHAT?

The pieces took 20,000 hours to put together.

20,000 hours. That's 833 days. Or 119 weeks. Or two years and three months.

After 67 million years underground, Sue moved to a super new home in one of America's great cities.

This is more like it.

Celebrity dinosaur

Sue arrived in pieces.

This is a tricky jigsaw ...

Did it come with any instructions?

HEAD

LEG

ARM

Sue soon got modern, and started using social media.*

*Not really: it's someone at the museum pretending.

REX means royalty you know.

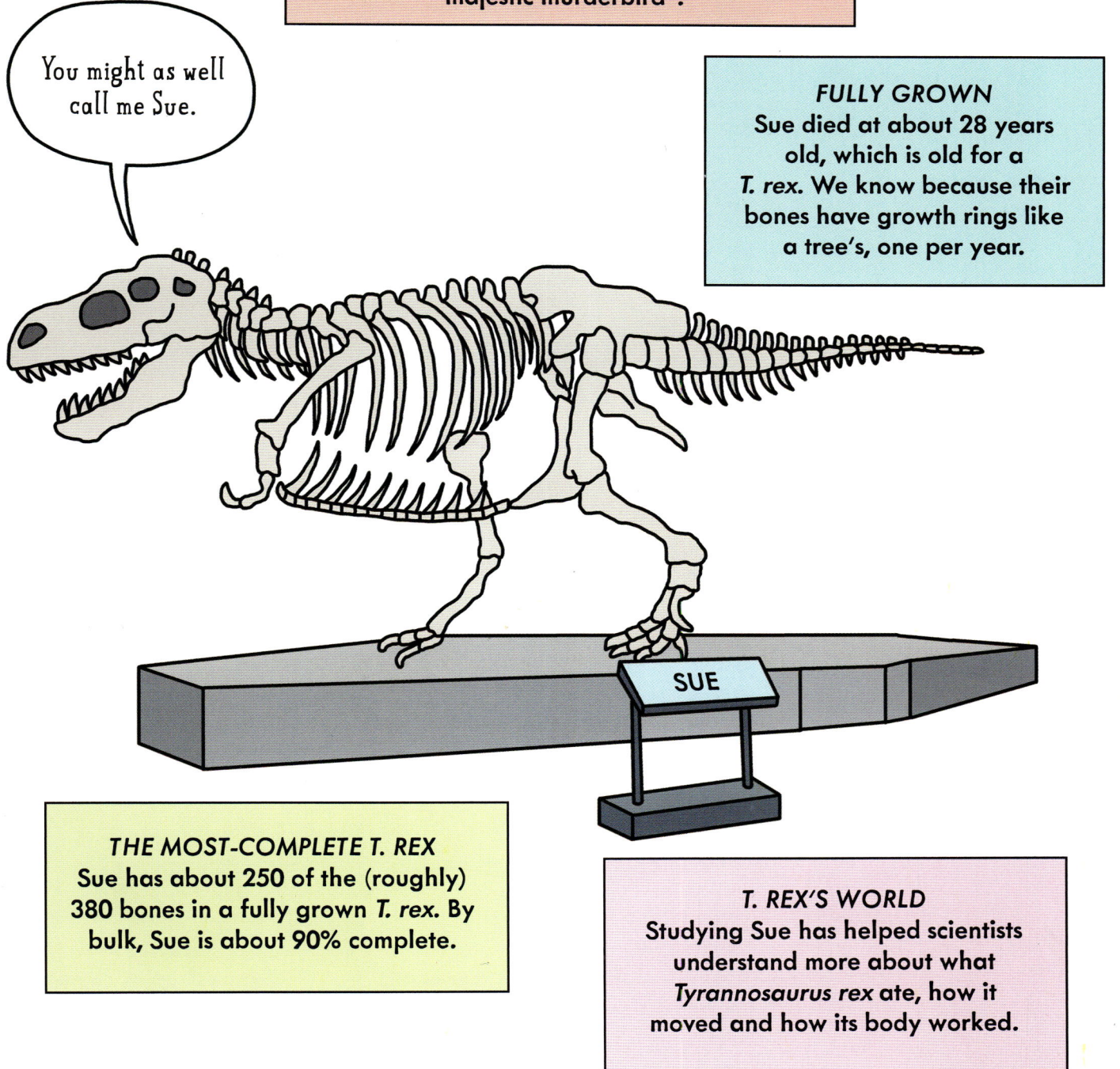

FEMALE OR MALE?
We don't know for sure if Sue was female or male — which led to this message on Sue's social media:

'My preferred pronouns are "they/them" ...

'As in, "SUE is a *T. rex*. They are a majestic murderbird".'

You might as well call me Sue.

FULLY GROWN
Sue died at about 28 years old, which is old for a *T. rex*. We know because their bones have growth rings like a tree's, one per year.

SUE

THE MOST-COMPLETE T. REX
Sue has about 250 of the (roughly) 380 bones in a fully grown *T. rex*. By bulk, Sue is about 90% complete.

T. REX'S WORLD
Studying Sue has helped scientists understand more about what *Tyrannosaurus rex* ate, how it moved and how its body worked.

DINOSAURS REIMAGINED

Many of the most exciting recent dinosaur discoveries have been in China – particularly in Liaoning Province.

Over 100 million years ago, Liaoning was a land of wide lakes and forests.

Dinosaurs, such as *Microraptor*, were not the only animals around.

Microraptor
SQUARK!
Nearly got him ...

There were mammals such as *Repenomamus* ...

The little ones are easy to catch.

That's what he thinks.

Nasty spines

... amphibians such as *Mesophryne** ...

RIBBET. RIBBET.

*Frogs have existed for 200 million years or more.

... and insects such as dragonflies and hornets.

So peaceful here.

ZZZZZZZZZZ!

Not any more.

The area often suffered from volcanic eruptions.

After an eruption, fine ash rained down.

The landscape was covered in a thick layer of ash.

For the wildlife of Liaoning, there was no escape.

Plants and animals were buried and died.

Below the ash layer, their bodies did not rot.

130 million years later, Liaoning has changed a lot ...

But the dinosaurs are still buried – sometimes quite near the surface.

One day, a farmer unearths an interesting-looking rock.

I wonder what this is?

DIG DIG

He finds an almost-perfect dinosaur, split in half.

And I thought being buried alive was bad ...

The two halves were eventually sold to different museums.

Other farmers begin to unearth fossilised remains.

This is much easier than actual farming.

Yes, isn't it.

The best fossils are bought by museums.

Soon, palaeontologists start to arrive in Liaoning.

This is where the fossils are?

Yep.

SIHETUN Dinosaur ~~City~~ Village

The fossils showed incredible details – even sometimes the dinosaur's last meal.

Smaller frog in stomach

Small dinosaur

One of the fossils was *Sinosauropteryx* – a small meat-eating dinosaur ... with feathers.

What's surprising about that?

Ever considered veganism?

Dinosaurs had feathers?

FEATHERS?

Dinosaur descendant

This was global news and helped confirm that modern birds were descended from dinosaurs!

1996, Heyuan city*: kids are playing near a building site.

What are these?

They look like stone eggs.

*in Southern China: important fossils have now been found in many parts of China.

They have found fossilised dinosaur eggs.

Many more – over 15,000 more – are later found.

That's really a LOT of eggs.

What did we start?

The discoveries at Liaoning have changed the way we see dinosaurs. The fossils are amazingly detailed. They show things palaeontologists have never seen before.

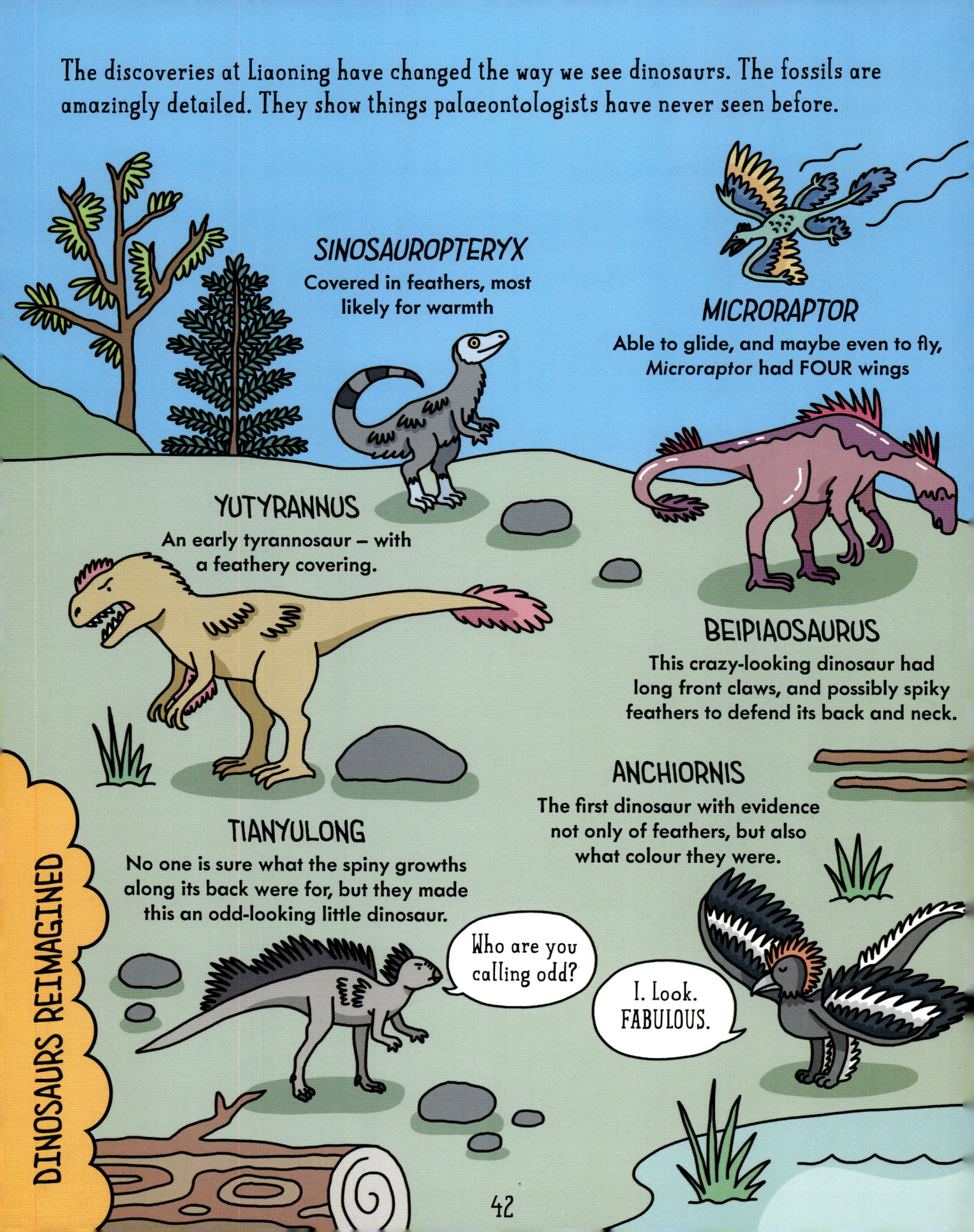

SINOSAUROPTERYX
Covered in feathers, most likely for warmth

MICRORAPTOR
Able to glide, and maybe even to fly, *Microraptor* had FOUR wings

YUTYRANNUS
An early tyrannosaur – with a feathery covering.

BEIPIAOSAURUS
This crazy-looking dinosaur had long front claws, and possibly spiky feathers to defend its back and neck.

ANCHIORNIS
The first dinosaur with evidence not only of feathers, but also what colour they were.

TIANYULONG
No one is sure what the spiny growths along its back were for, but they made this an odd-looking little dinosaur.

Who are you calling odd?

I. Look. FABULOUS.

DINOSAURS REIMAGINED

The Liaoning fossils also tell us more than ever about the world dinosaurs lived in, and the animals and plants they shared it with.

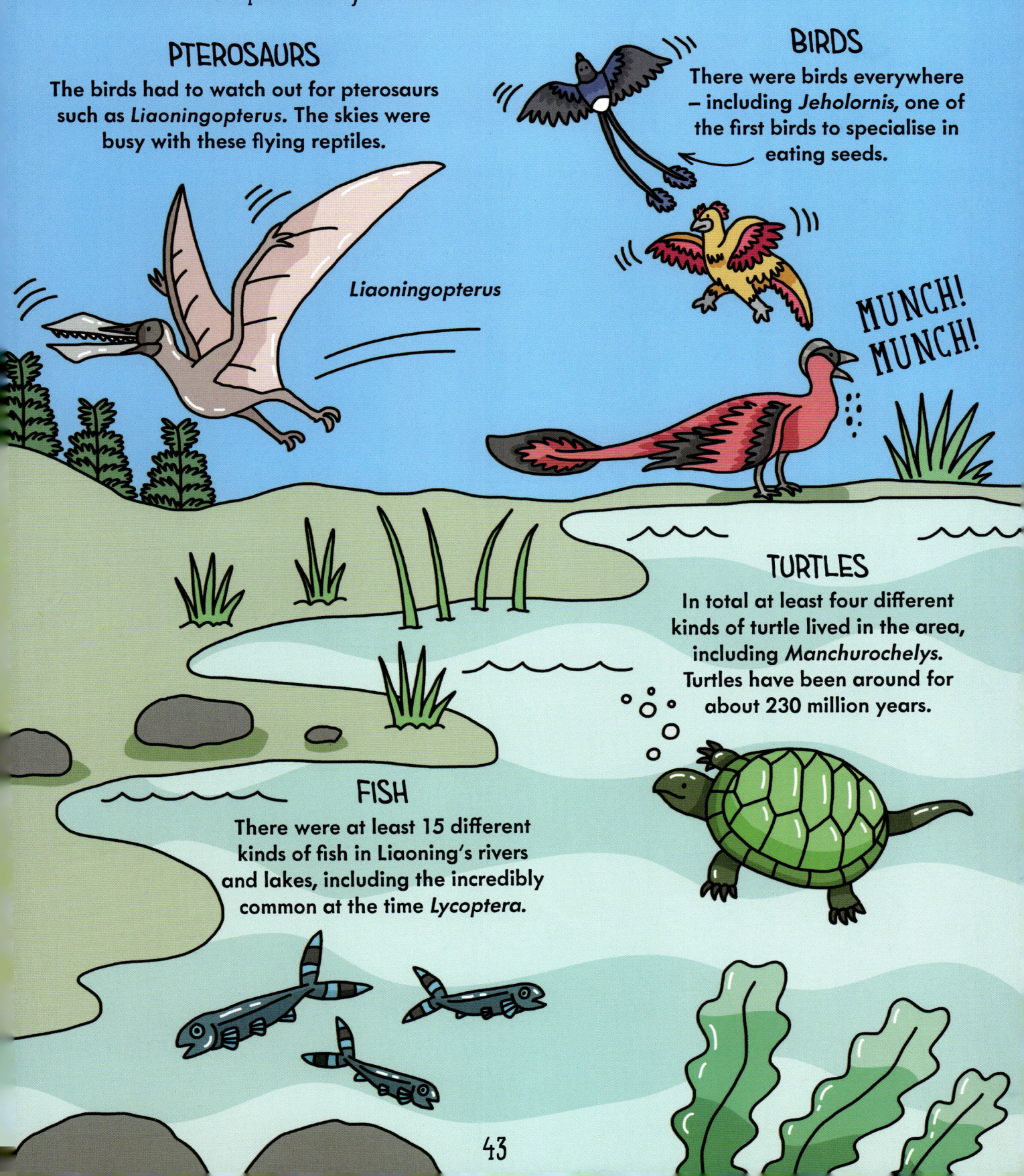

PTEROSAURS

The birds had to watch out for pterosaurs such as *Liaoningopterus*. The skies were busy with these flying reptiles.

Liaoningopterus

BIRDS

There were birds everywhere – including *Jeholornis*, one of the first birds to specialise in eating seeds.

MUNCH! MUNCH!

TURTLES

In total at least four different kinds of turtle lived in the area, including *Manchurochelys*. Turtles have been around for about 230 million years.

FISH

There were at least 15 different kinds of fish in Liaoning's rivers and lakes, including the incredibly common at the time *Lycoptera*.

43

RECONSTRUCTING DINOSAURS

Once palaeontologists have unearthed a new dinosaur, they try to work out what it might have looked like.

1. SKELETON AND STANCE

The first thing to work out is what shape the dinosaur was and how it stood. Did it stand on two legs, four or both?

Sometimes this is not clear. Over the years, experts have disagreed about how *Spinosaurus* stood, for example. Today it is thought to have used its back legs.

| 1920s *Spinosaurus* | 1990s *Spinosaurus* | 2020s *Spinosaurus* |

RAAR!

On two legs

On four legs

Back on two legs

2. BODY SHAPE

Experts can tell from fossils where the dinosaur had the biggest muscles and the strongest bones. This tells them where it was probably biggest and the ways it moved.

Megalosaurus was the first dinosaur ever to be described in writing. Soon afterwards it was drawn – but today's *Megalosaurus* looks like a completely different animal ...

Hello, I'm *Megalosaurus*.

I don't think you are.

1850s *Megalosaurus*

1990s *Megalosaurus*

3. GIVE THE DINOSAUR SKIN. AND MAYBE FEATHERS.

People used to think that all dinosaurs had skin like lizards or crocodiles. But then fossils began to show us that some had feathers.

Yutyrannus, a tyrannosaur from northern China, seems to have had feathers over most of its body. They probably helped it keep warm.

Oh, the weather outside is frightful ...

Yutyrannus

Today, scientists can compare fossils to other dinosaurs and to similar animals that still exist. As a result, we know more about what the world of dinosaurs looked like than ever before.

DINOSAUR QUIZ

1. WHAT WERE THE BONE WARS?

a) a famous battle between rival gangs of skeletons in a graveyard at midnight

b) a bitter rivalry between two US palaeontologists

c) an epic refusal by Charles McGruder, aged 9, to go to the broken-bones clinic at hospital after falling out of a tree.

2. WHY WAS THE WORLD'S MOST EXPENSIVE DINOSAUR CALLED SUE?

a) because that's what her parents named her

b) she chose it herself, as she had always admired the music of American rock star Suzi Quatro

c) the person who discovered Sue's fossil remains was called Sue.

3. IN LIAONING, CHINA, SOME FARMERS FOUND:

a) avocados

b) dinosaur fossils

c) gold and diamonds.

4. WHERE WERE DINOSAUR EGGS FIRST FOUND?

a) in a dinosaur nest, obviously

b) in the Gobi Desert

c) both of the above.

5. MARY ANNING'S FAVOURITE TRAY WAS:

a) the tea tray used by her mum to bring her tea and crumpets

b) her fossil-hunting dog called Tray

c) the tray on which fossils were displayed in her fossil shop.

6. DINOSAURS HAD SCALY SKIN LIKE A SNAKE'S: TRUE OR FALSE?

a) true

b) false

c) it's not that simple: sometimes true, sometimes not.

7. IS A FOSSIL:

a) someone so old-fashioned they still have a black-and-white TV*

b) the remains of a living thing that have turned to stone

c) a dinosaur that has been dug up?

*These did actually exist, honestly.

8. WHAT DID *SPINOSAURUS* LIKE BEST FOR DINNER?

a) takeaway curry (*Oviraptor* vindaloo was its absolute favourite)

b) raw fish

c) baked *Anchiornis*.

The answers are on page 48.

DINOSAUR GLOSSARY

air pen air-powered device about the size of a thick pen, which works a bit like a dentist's drill

ammonite curly-shaped fossil of a shelled sea creature that lived millions of years ago. They looked a bit like squid, with a hard, curly shell

eruption sudden explosion, particularly of lava and ash from a volcano

eye socket part of the skull containing the eyeball

lava liquid rock from deep within Earth, which has come to the surface because of volcanic activity

mammal animal that can feed its young with milk from the mother

mineral non-living material that is found in nature, often buried underground and contained in rock or soil

palaeontologist someone who studies fossilised animals and plants as a way of learning about the past

plesiosaur reptile from the time of the dinosaurs that lived in water. Plesiosaurs were not dinosaurs

remains parts left over after other parts have been destroyed or lost. So, the remains of a sandwich might be some crusts, while the remains of a tyrannosaur might be a huge skull, some teeth or even a whole skeleton

rockfall sudden fall of loose rocks from a cliff face

stance how something stands. If you stand with your feet far apart, that's a wide stance. With your feet close together, you have a narrow stance

tyrannosaur one of a group of large, meat-eating dinosaurs that includes *Albertosaurus*, *Tarbosaurus* and (of course) *Tyrannosaurus rex*

vegan eating or using no animals or animal products (such as milk)

volcanic ash fine ash produced when a volcano erupts

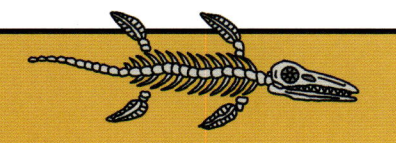

INDEX

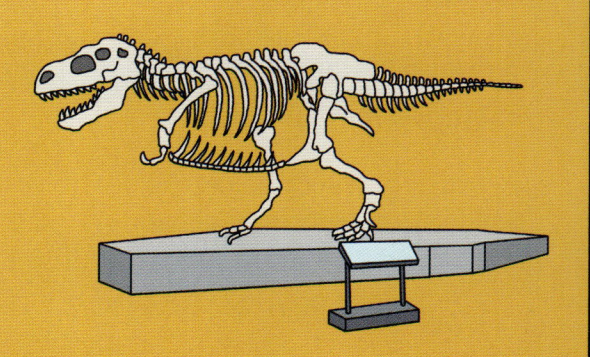

QUIZ ANSWERS

1 b): rival palaeontologists, E D Cope and O C Marsh, uncovered lots of dinosaur fossils;
2 c): they named Sue after the person who discoverd the dinosaur; 3 b): fossils;
4 b): although some dinosaurs did lay their eggs in nests, too; 5 b): Tray was the name
of Mary Anning's dog; 6 c): we now know that dinosaurs had various skin coverings and
colours; 7 b): (dinosaurs are not the only things that died and were fossilised: plants and
other animals did too); 8 b): (cooking was off the menu, as it would not be invented for
several million years).